To: Antonia!
Your suppo
Great Su

show.

Much love,

Jt C. H-
8/15

# LIFE, LOVE & GOD

## LLG: Poetry Collection Volume One

### Justin C. Hart

## #1 Inspirational Bestselling Author

*3G Publishing, Inc.*
*3600 Park Lake Lane*
*Norcross, Georgia 30092*
*www.3gpublishinginc.com*
*Phone: 1-888-442-9637*

*First published by 3G Publishing, Inc., January, 2013*

*ISBN: 978-0-9833544-8-2*

*Printed in the United States of America*

## ~ *Dedication* ~

I dedicate this *LLG: Life, Love & God Poetry Collection* to my gorgeous wife, Jasmine, my parents, and every God-given individual, friend, and poet that has encouraged me as a writer. I appreciate you all from the center of my heart. A special thanks to my 2010 LLG Men's Group at Victory World Church in Atlanta, Georgia.  You are the *original* LLG!

*Together*
*Life is not so complicated*
*Forever*
*Love should be re-instated*
*God's grace is so amazing*
*The cumulous clouds read painted...*

*Life, Love & God*

Justin C. Hart

# ~ *Contents* ~

# ~ *LIFE* ~

# ~ *LOVE* ~

# ~ *GOD* ~

## *An Endless Appreciation to...*

My Lord. My Savior. My Image. My Lineage.
My Big Brother. My Provider. My Rock. My Doctor.
My Healer. My Sanctifier. My Creator.
My Promise Keeper.
My Shepherd. My Lion. My Lamb. The Son of Man.
My Redeemer. My Deliverer. My Compass. My Constant. My
Joy. My Peace. My King. My Everything.
My Commander in Chief. Jesus!

I Worship You...

## ~ *LLG Preface* ~

This collection of poetry that rests before your eyes span from the curious, and often times prideful age of 18, to the more wisdom-filled and humble age of 29. I have been privileged to obtain a particular gift and love for writing since my childhood and it is an honor to share my inner thoughts, emotions, and experiences with the world; particularly you, my friend.

By the grace of God, there was no better time for me to have written this book. I had been prompted by Him to gather my poetry over the last decade and categorize them into three of my most dynamic living experiences: Life, Love, and God. I have found that there is no greater cluster of impactful words within our daily vocabulary than these three. I am truly grateful for this gift of writing and I anticipate all that God has in store for me... especially with this treasure of poetry.

May this first volume become timeless food for your soul...

Mommy, Daddy
Mommy, Daddy, Me
Mommy, Me
Mommy, where did Daddy go?
He's working all this week…

## LITTLE WHITE LIES…

Daddy, Mommy
Daddy, Mommy, Me
Daddy, Me
Daddy, where did Mommy go?
She's playing hide and seek…

## ~ 6 SENSES ~

**All I Know** is the Lord, family, school, girls, my true friends, jewelry, sports, and this small, small world. **All I See** is love, hate, crimes, dimes, and nudity, backstabbers, liars, criers, and people looking down on me. **All I Hear** is voices with fear and cheer. Folks talking about alcohol, beer, weed, and cuss words that start fatal dares. I can't bear knowing that **All I Feel** is God's presence and His chills up my spine, like a girl's soft touch – Yo, what's the deal? I know all the hate and love I feel is real, because once something good happens I want seconds just like a good meal. And when something bad happens, I can mentally and physically feel it, just like braille. **All I Smell** is backyard cookouts and food from down south, bad breath coming from the mouth, perfume, and herbal smoke. I must have a good snout. **All I Taste** is rice and chicken, toothpaste, and Mistics; dryness, never mind this, because everything I've spoken is realistic. While you have the fortune, remember I'm keeping the fame. When negative things happen, God isn't the one to blame. I have five senses; the sixth one has been sought. The more I pursue after it, the more I am taught. It's called discernment.

It took us four years to get through it
And we got through it together
Same days different weather
Same jeans different sweaters, whatever

We went from knowing no one, to everyone knowing us
Going down together when one of us would get caught cussing
I'm not fussing at y'all/ Y'all were my crew
And you can't get mad if there were more than you

My other crew, my teammates, my unprofessional sports figures
We posted along that hallway wall like no one was bigger
From September to June, morning to noon
We stuck together through the years as we watched
ourselves bloom

Both of my crews had their own wall
That's called territory/ We had to own it all

Girls, would go out of their way just to get their backs on it
Whoever was hot at the time/ Yeah, they wanted their hands on
him/ Girls would come and go, and I'd remain saying, "Hi." But
when one of my partners would come and go... I'd go out of my
way just to say, "Bye. Catch you later. Take it easy. Stay up."
Until the next day comes...

**TO MY OLD FRIENDS...**

## ONCE UPON A TIME

My Buds were light
Crazy college kid
My hugs were tight

I used to go party hoppin'
My nights were late
Sippin' to get it poppin'
A large crew, no dates

Acting wild to the music
No home training
Teaching others how we do it
Our dance steps were amazing

Once upon a time
The club life was it
But once I started growing up
I had to call it quits

### First Corinthians - Eleven: Thirteen

*"When I was a child, I spoke as a child; I thought as a child; I did childish things. But when I became a man, I put my childish ways behind me."*

**THAT LIL' BOY** who once cried when he was hungry...
Now stands as a man, fully understanding the need for spiritual food.

That lil' boy who once threw tantrums when his way wasn't granted... Now stands as a man, fully responsible for controlling his moods.

That lil' boy who once played for hours with his toys...
Now stands as a man, working hard to pay bills on time.

That lil' boy who once was so innocent and pure...
Now stands as a man, continuously having to renew his tainted mind.

That lil' boy who once ran when he was fearful...
Now stands as a man, fully embracing the word courage.

That lil' boy who once stuttered when he spoke...
Now stands as a man, testifying with fluency before churches.

That lil' boy who wanted to run away from home...
Now stands as a man, being the head of his own.

That lil' boy who once thought about committing suicide...
Now stands as a man, telling others don't.

# L.O.S.T.

Looking for love in all the wrong places led me down a path of lies and lukewarm lovers that couldn't satisfy my longing to be loved like I had longed to be - before my birth I lustfully laid in my mother's womb so comfortably living without the leeches of the world latching onto my soul, laughing out loud would ultimately distract my knowledge of being lost,
yet I was.

Obviously I was oblivious to my circumstances while others noticed overtly that I opted to walk around foolishly speaking omitted words from my empty heart that had only repeated bias objections which created offenses due to my lack of understanding of being lost, yet I was.

Sorry Mom and Dad for silently and sinfully slaughtering the hope that you instilled inside of this mind of mine while I was sitting under your sugar coated ginger bread roof slothfully making sudden moves to better my situation so now I shamefully sit here and shrink within my shell doubting myself wondering why I can't remain sober while being lost,
yet I do.

There were times when the second-hand of time struck like terrible lightning and taunted me like a ticking time bomb touching the texture of my skin that I hated so much which somehow destined me to throw text onto torn paper in lieu of tantrums while all along my true identity that I always knew existed awaited to be found and thank You, Jesus, it was.

## PEOPLE

Look
Look around
Look left, look right, look up, look down
Look at all the people you just found
Look when you walk
Look when you ride
Look how they run
Look how they drive
Look at their faces
Look at their hair
Look at their smiles
Look but don't stare
Look at their struggles
Look at their tears
Look at their frustrations
You've been looking for years
You've been looking for too long
You look but do nothing
Look at all the hurting people
Now is the time to do something

## TERRIBLE THOUGHTS

I know this is terrible, but...

I've contemplated suicide more than I should admit

The devil has implanted terrible thoughts in my head
as a kid

I've thought about calling it quits, time and time again

And my life isn't even terrible...

My heart goes out to you, if your life has been...

## TEARS

One night I realized tears weren't clear
Cried they dripped slightly red
They were inner wounds from disappointments
Blood-like tears ever-flowing shed
Soaked until pain yelled pain
But agony replaced it instead
Watered couch with tears cried often
Puddles nearby surrounded bed
Tissues nor sleeves nor handkerchiefs were enough
Weightiness from eyes hung head
Longing for liberation ached seeking soul
My, my, my emotions dancing but were dead
Jesus wept then shall I
Tears crocodile by ruined stale bread
Once I heard man cannot live on bread only
Forever God's spoken words, Jesus said

Tears zero since then

## SRAET

Clear weren't tears realized I night one
Red slightly dripped they cried
Disappointments from wounds inner were they
Shed ever-flowing tears like blood
Pain yelled pain until soaked
Instead it replaced agony but
Often cried tears with couch watered
Bed surrounded by near puddles
Enough weren't handkerchiefs nor sleeves nor tissues
Head hung eyes from weightiness
Soul seeking, ached liberation for longing
Dead were but dancing emotions, my, my, my
I shall, then wept Jesus
Bread stale, ruined by crocodile tears
Only bread, man cannot live, heard I once
Said Jesus, words spoken, God's forever

Then since, zero tears

**IT IS WHAT IT IS**

Times are changing
Rearranging
My life that is
Which is so amazing

Memories are fading
Last year went blazing
Fast that is
My heart's still racing

Patience is strong from waiting
My money is chasing
Me that is
And it's far from wasting

My roof is raising
Future kids are tasting
Food that is
Their bellies are craving

Provision is staying
Our home is remaining
Here that is
No more complaining

## LIFE LESSON #1 – IDENTITY

Of late, I complain about wisdom not being passed from generation to generation. So I figure, there is nothing stopping me from sharing valuable education with this younger nation. You see a majority of youth do not have good fathers to train them. And those irresponsible fathers more than likely had fathers that unfortunately defamed them. So, I'm slower than I am quick to judge another man's current lacking, because best believe there is lacking within the lacking. See what's happening is there is a loss of identity. If I asked, "Who are you?" Could you answer me? So many of us are flaunting fake ID's, acting as fictional characters, and accepting our man-made mask as who our Creator created us to be. But I say directly to you – you are one decision away from being a child of God; inheritance and all. Pause, think about that. Don't make it hard. Once you accept Jesus, God's Son as the Lord and Savior of your life, you also become a son or daughter. That's why we call God, Father. I love that part! This is a foundational truth. This is the seed of who you are. All the things this deceptive world labels you as, it won't matter anymore. Of late, you complain about wisdom not being passed from generation to generation. So I figure, what's stopping *you* from sharing valuable education with this younger nation? You see a majority of youth do not have good fathers to train them. And those irresponsible fathers more than likely had fathers that unfortunately defamed them. So, be slower than you are quick to judge another man's current lacking, because best believe there is lacking within the lacking. But now, our fake identities are no longer laughing. And I'm so happy.

## LIFE LESSON #2 – PURPOSE

Recently, I'm frustrated about understanding not being understood from generation to generation. Then I thought, there's nothing keeping me from speaking the truth to this deceptive nation. You see a multitude of teenagers do not have good mothers to learn from. And those incomplete mothers more than likely didn't have whole mothers to teach them. So, I'm passionate more than I am passive towards young women and reaching them, because best believe there is understanding lacking within the understanding. See what's happening is there is a loss of purpose. I must ask you, "Do your sons and daughters know their worth yet?" Therefore, it's a race for their soul's purchase. Who will win, the world or Christ? We've already been ransomed. We've been bought with a price. We had a blood donor step up 2000 plus years ago just so we could live. Jesus died for our sins. Our heavenly Father made amends. If parenthood doesn't motivate you to become a better parent than your parents, then it's apparent that your purpose isn't clear yet. Your job is to be on fire for God's Kingdom and live passionately for the King. Since He died for me, I will live for Him. Our purpose is found within. We won't be lost again! Still, recently you're frustrated about understanding not being understood from generation to generation. Then I thought, what's keeping *you* from speaking the truth to this deceptive nation? You see a multitude of teenagers do not have good mothers to learn from. And those incomplete mothers more than likely didn't have whole mothers to teach them. So, be passionate more than you are passive towards young women and reaching them. And all we needed was one reason. Jesus. Done!

## LIFE LESSON #3 – DIRECTION

Lately, I bicker about knowledge not being passed from generation to generation. Yet, I'm speechless as to why I don't verbally share scripture with this rebellious nation. You see a large percentage of people do not have good friends to look up to. And their foolish friends more than likely do not have good friends to sit down with. So, I'm quicker than I am slow to politely correct another man's knowledge, because best believe there is knowledge lacking within the knowledge. See what's happening is there is a loss of direction. If I asked, "Where are you going?" Could you name your destination? The large number of souls that are walking the wide path are all lost. Too many folks following the crowd and they don't know the cost. You want directions young people? Listen to The Boss. It's not me, but He who died on the cross. He is The One who arose and directs the steps of the righteous. It is He who breathes life into the lifeless. It is He who we are following until the end. Simply follow me as I follow Him. Lately, you bicker about knowledge not being passed from generation to generation. Yet, you're speechless as to why *you* don't verbally share scripture with this rebellious nation. You see a large percentage of people do not have good friends to look up to. And their foolish friends more than likely do not have good friends to sit down with. So, be quicker than you are slow to politely correct another man's knowledge, because best believe there is knowledge lacking within the knowledge. See what's happening is there is a loss of direction. And I know I'm not perfect, but I know where to find perfection. Let's go!

Money, cheese, cheddar, dough          $$$$$$$
Green, paper, steady cash flow
A grip, a stack, a wad, some lettuce
My cut, my tip, please don't spend it

If cents make dollars
Then dollars make sense
But it doesn't make sense
To lose your sense over dollars

I used to worry
Cry and freak out over funds
Or the lack there of
There's no fun with ones

I've been receiving
Unemployment checks
Far too long... I need a job
Can you help me, Mom!?

Money, moolah, bills, bucks
Cream, cabbage, no chips, no luck
A pound, a knot, some bread, some bacon
My stash, my loot, a hot date – she's paying          $$$$$$$

Do u really gotta have it?
The next toy - the next gadget...
01010101110010100100101101010000
But do u really need it?
Another game to hit reset...
00001010101111010010101111110
Do u really want it?
The newest phone with voice text...

**TECHNOLOGY**

10101110101101010000101011010101010110
But can u live without it?
Your 50 inch flat screen - I doubt it...
1011011010010100000010100101010110001
What if someone took it?
Your iPad and booked it...
11111101010000101010100010
What if someone broke it?
Your iPhone, then smoked it...
Lit it on fire, threw it on the ground and choked it...
10010010011110000101001011110011010100010101010111101
Stop wasting money on things!
Especially if u can't afford
To accomplish your own dreams...
10100111101001001001000001010101100
Technology doesn't love u, Jack.
Only upgrade if it's paying u back.
Nice Mac...

Have you travelled the world yet?
Have you been to Tibet?

Have you been to Cuba, Brazil, or Paris, France
Where they speak French?

How about Jamaica, Puerto Rico, or Japan?
Thailand or Egypt?

Why don't we all take a summer trip
to the Mother Land or Fiji?

Have you been along the coast of Mexico or Florida?

Please say you've at least visited New York or California

At least Georgia or Virginia, one or the other

You said, *You haven't left your state yet?*

Let me talk to your mother!

**VACATION!**

You are living
But so far from being alive
I'll consider you the living dead
Your heart has withered and died
But I'm going to speak life until your dry bones comply
Let's go on a ride within your mind
Simply close your eyes and set aside
Those distracting thoughts that seem to arrive
You can kiss them all goodbye
And kiss hello - Your pot of gold
Your riches are plentiful - What a sight to behold!
My destiny is your slightest decision
YOU ARE ME in twenty years
Listen closely as I guide with wisdom
The fork in the road is just as it appears
Your purpose, identity, and direction
Have been lost, but will be found
Don't allow your dirty past
To cripple you to the dirty ground
This day, choose life and stand up
Regain the great hope that sustains
Your future is not your past
Your faith in God still remains
Remove your left foot from the grave
**YOU'RE ALIVE, I SAY! LIVE!**
Live like you have never lived before
Sing until your voice becomes hoarse
Play in the crashing waves along the private shore
Dance until your feet become sore - LIVE!
Live like true love is brand new
Write like a poet would write at forty-two
Run like champions run when they're in a good mood
Laugh hard until your cheeks hurt, too
LIVE! You're alive, I say! LIVE!

## REMEMBER WHEN THIS WAS LOVE?

Remember when this was love, when you and your friends
would talk about what you were going to do over the
summer while it was still spring?

---

Remember when this was love, when the last day of school came
and you would get tight hugs from all the people you
wouldn't see anymore?

---

Remember when this was love, when you would be outside with
your best friends from sun up
until the street light?

---

Remember when this was love, when you would play catch with
your grandpa, dad, uncle, brother, cousin,
or best friend?

---

Remember when this was love, when you and your friends
would ride bikes all day and drink Kool-Aid or water from
the hose whenever you got thirsty?

---

Remember when this was love, when you and your best friend
thought about building a treehouse
or secret hiding spot?

Remember when this was love,
when friendship had no color?

-------------------------------------------------------------------------

Remember when this was love, when you actually had a
good time hanging out with your family?

-------------------------------------------------------------------------

Remember when this was love, when you would start a
game and it wouldn't end for a couple of days later?

-------------------------------------------------------------------------

Remember when this was love, when it didn't matter what the
score was, you were just playing a game that you
loved?

-------------------------------------------------------------------------

Remember when this was love, when a house party was
coincidentally started by the sound of old school music
and the smell of a barbeque grill?

-------------------------------------------------------------------------

Remember when this was love, when colored water balloons,
super soakers, and buckets of water turned into
hours worth of wet fun?

-------------------------------------------------------------------------

Remember when this was love?

I do...

*. . . LOVE*

# LOVE ...

Should love be one of the Seven Wonders of the World? I know it could be. Who can truly understand the actions and feelings of love, besides God in heaven who created it? From my experiences, which you will read shortly, my life has been impacted more by the heartaches of love than by the headaches of life. My heart has fallen in and out of love numerous times, entangled with sin, only to be purified permanently by my decision to love God first and foremost. God is my first priority and people and things are second, third and so on. This is what love should look like; however, my love life has not always looked like this. Often times the ranking was backwards and God reigned in strong second, or third. Can you relate? Good, I'm glad I am not the only one with my hand raised...

This is my poetry collection of LOVE ... Enjoy.

## LOVE IS LOVE …

Is love you? Is love me?
Is love what I show for you in your time of need?
Can love be shown mentally? Spiritually? Physically?
Intimately is how lovers show love. Permanently is how
brothers show love. Eternally is how God shows love.
Unconditionally is how God loves thugs.
Continuously is how thugs should love God.
If you can overstand my thoughts then just nod.

Is love cars? Is love money?
Is lust the love that we have for these clothes-less
Playboy bunnies?
Isn't it funny how we love to live double lives?
On Sunday we're sinless, but by Friday night we're at the
Gentlemen's Club, "gettin' right." Do we love sin, but hate
the consequences? The consequence of sin is
death by the way, I forgot to mention.

Is love food? Is love an icon? Is love the attraction that you have
for a woman with nice legs and a man with nice
arms? Is the love for sports and entertainment the same
love you show towards the family and friends that you're
claiming? It's a shame when we become addicted to
earthly things, tempted by Satan. All the everlasting things
provided by God we should cherish.
Look at all the time that we are wasting.

For God so loved the world
that He gave His only begotten son. Jesus is His name.
He is heaven's only bright sun.
The Lord's love for us is the true definition of love.
We can't fathom why God loves us so much.
Honestly, I've never seen Him
and He's never been touched;
but I know how He feels.
That's deep, huh? Just nod if I'm keeping it real.

I love speaking with God. I love relating with Jesus.
I love having the Holy Spirit living within me during all
four seasons; during every troublesome time and season
of my life, for no reason. Correction, I hope my apology is
accepted. The reason is God's love.
In time of need, have you ever experienced one of God's
hugs? It's like a peaceful, soothing, and relaxing spiritual
flood. May we take communion, break the bread, and
symbolically drink of Jesus' blood? If the pace of my
passion is too fast for you, then you must not let the devil's
secondhand smoke destroy your lungs.
My tongue is one that speaks love into the ears of many.
Many love the fact that my tongue speaks clearly.
In closing, love is love…
God loves us more than plenty.

## HER NAME WAS MUSIC

I heard her in the morning
She woke me up with her melody
      Her rhythm beat on my soul
      And stole my attention like a felony
I got lost in her acoustics
Her sound was like my medicine
      I increased her volume often
      Overdosing on my friend again
She had fans around the world
She created a vibe ever-present
      I let her whisper in my ears
      I loved her verbal and nonverbal messages
Occasionally, I pulled up a chair
Sat there with my eyes closed
      I heard my lady out
      Feeling like my mind was blown
She had a unique style
It changed every time I would choose it
      She was my first lover
      Above all others ... Her name was Music

**BREAK UP TO MAKE UP** - That's all we do
We've broken up five times in eight months
This love can't be true
Am I being deceived for something that it's not?
Are you a coldhearted woman who claims to be hot?
I'm a contentious man, even more so at night
Are you my Miss Wrong,
Convincingly dressed up as Miss Right?
And now we've fallen for each other
How do we know if it's real?
Even the clouds cry
So tears aren't the main meal
Tears are the appetizer
They satisfy my appetite
The love I have for you is my hunger
Tear drops won't suffice
Satisfy my starvation
My desire to be fed
You're feeding me table scraps
Do you understand what I just said?
Sharing your feelings towards me
Puts a smile in my ears
Seeing what you've done to me
Brings back bad memories from past years
Your actions mean more to me than all of the above
The devil can tell me he loves me
But I know that's not God's love
Truth isn't always what someone tells you
Truth should be crystal clear
Your tears tell me you love me
But unfortunately that's not what I hear...

**The old me** used to whisper into the ears of some pretty young thangs/I used to tell them sweet thangs that they wanted to hear/Persuasion invasion/My flirtation used to lure them into the nearest Days Inn/Touching, teasing, teaching, pleasing/**The old me** used to do certain things with no reasoning/Like sprinkling seasoning on her bones for flavor/**The old me** was in need of a Savior/I used to laugh at sin/Diving nose first when I'd swim/Back stroke slow when I'd stroke her back/As a matter of fact, I'd cut my phone off so folks wouldn't know where I was at/Midnight – twilight – sunrise/Staring at her face until she opened her eyes/**The old me** used to lie/I would lie to the girls I was laying with like I was wearing a disguise/My pride wouldn't let me hide/The thoughts I kept inside ate me alive/**The old me** is old/Ancient/History/Prehistoric/I'm stepping on the gas pedal/Watch me floor it/I'm leaving my lustful ways in the past/I continue to pass temptation, praying that it never comes back/Thank You, Lord for deliverance/You own my inheritance in heaven and I know it's not a little bit/A big settlement is what I've been promised, kid/**The old me** used to break girls' hearts/Tear them apart/And not even care/Not even wipe their tears/I was gone/I wouldn't even tell them so long/I was wrong/But I finally found the right words for this song/Not only have I changed, but I have been re-born/Jesus, Your hands do more than transform/The new me is here/**THE OLD ME IS GONE!**

**[ I AM PATIENTLY WAITING**
**I am not in a rush**
**When God feels I'm ready**
**I will find true love ]**
Should I keep my eyes open
And embrace the one that puts a smile in my eyes?
Or should I keep my eyes closed and have the touch
Of the one relieve me from being blind?
Should I search for my Queen
Or have my Queen find her King?
Should I whisper sweet things
Or keep my feelings bottled in dreams?
Lord, I know You know
Lord, You have to know
Still I'm patiently waiting
To find a mate for my soul
To find a soft voice for my songs
To find a replacement for my yawns
To find a woman like my mom
To find a woman that is strong
I am willing to wait, Lord
But I don't know for how long…

I thought I would be married by now - How?

Who?
    What?
        When?
            Where?
                Why aren't you standing next to me?

Why aren't you texting me, my future spouse?

I thought I would be married by now... Another birthday
celebrated with all my friends
and their significant others

Only my mother strengthens my hope about finding
the right lover

My father, sister, and brother tell me to stay focused
on my career

But they are not here to count my single man tears


**IT'S BEEN 5 YEARS!**

## ALL OF A SUDDEN

It's just a look
It's just a glance
It could be as simple
As a simple pass

It's just a touch
It's just a rub
It could be as simple
As a simple hug

And then suddenly…

It's just a thought
It's just a breath
It could be as simple
As as simple gets

It's just a drink
It's just a glass
It could be as simple
As a simple laugh

And then suddenly…

It's just a smile
It's just a sniff
It could be as simple
As a simple gift

It's just a dream
It's just a memory
It could be as simple
As a simple melody

And then suddenly…

Before you know it
You're in love,
Love, love, love

All over again
You're in love
And you don't know
Where it came from

You're in love

And then suddenly,
You're in love

## LOVE LOST AND FOUND

I found you
You found me
Love lost and found
Sweeter than Georgia sweet tea
On a Sunday evening
I saw a young lady in front of me
Sweeter than honey from a bumble bee
She resembled a woman named Beverly
Oooohhhh, Beverly
Sweeter than sap from a tree
She spoke to me
Words lighter than the air I breathe
And she said to me,
"Wow... Hello stranger.
Where have you been?
It's been so many years.
Do you remember who I am?"
"To be honest,
You look like an old friend.
But, I wouldn't be that lucky to bump into her again."
"Well, I think your luck is beginning to change.
I know you remember me,
I'm Beverly..."

"Oh my goodness, it's been so long.
You still look amazing.
Are you in town for the holidays?
Do you still live on Main Street?"
"Yes, I still live in the city.
And yes, I still live on Main.
And you're still looking good, too.
I see you haven't changed."
"I've changed a lot,
More so internally.
But what are you doing now?
You wanna get some hot tea
With me,
Beverly?"
Ooohhhh, Beverly
Such a sweet name
Bringing back sweet memories
I found you
You found me
Love lost and found

You know I try hard to not get my hopes up
But with you, it seems like I have no luck
Scripture says, "Be anxious for nothing," and I know this
Yet I'm anxious everyday - I hope you don't notice
What we have to look forward to is very special
I've never called anyone *My Future,* except you
Why do I smile when you look at me?
You're my friend,
And a friend shouldn't make me feel this way
I get chills and thrills, then my heart jumps
I'm a grown man listening to my heart thump
It's confirmed
I'm ready to move forward in pursuit of you
The pursuit of happiness
Is only pursued by a chosen few
Me and you - You and I - It feels so right
A collection of poems are waiting for you
In the corner of my mind
Hoping that one day - all of you - would be all of mine
But like I said, I try hard to not get my hopes up
Still I hope for the day we can hold our toasts up…

**LOVE, YOUR FRIEND**

### STRANGE WOMAN (SHE IS)

She is the reason why I sin
The one who has me lusting again, She is
She is the ink in my pen
The one who has me writing again, She is
She is the thorn in my flesh
The one who turns my no to yes, She is
She is the apple in my eye
The one who dries my tears when I cry, She is
She is the wrong to my right
The one who turns off my light, She is
She is the right to my wrong
The one who makes me feel like I belong, She is
She is the touches and the rubs
The one who makes temptation come, She is
She is the loving hugs
The one who loves the Creator above, She is
She is not found in my future
The one that works at Hooters, She is
She is a big part of my life
The one that's soon to be my wife, She is

## CLEAR SKIES

Smile, you're beautiful
You plus me equals suitable
Suitability – I like that
We complement each other like a dome in a hat
What'd you say? You think I'm fly?
Girl, you're flier than me – Let's go on and get high
Not high from the plants in the ground you see
But high like the peaks of the trees with falling leaves
We can breeze through the evergreens and never sneeze
We can glide to the other side - Nah, never mind
I like where I have you – Stay right here
I like where you have me – Girl, don't stare
Keep your hands right there – You're not playing fair
We have to stay pure - Before the Lord
He knows our every thought – It is in His Word
If we're going to play this game – Let's play it together
Same rule book, coach, and strategy forever
Foreplay and foul play are all the same – Be clever
Clear skies in the forecast – I want good weather
We're rocking no sweaters
Why are you still making me sweat?
My name ain't Keith, girl – The 10th letter knows best!

## SIMPLE

I'm a simple man
I want to live a simple life
Marry a simple wife
So we can simply spend 40 simple days and 40 simple
nights/ *A 40 day honeymoon?* You ask/ Simple
I'm 10x four men, plus she has dimples
She's light skin with dark brown eyes/ Nice thighs
A simple smile that makes me go simply wild
*How did you meet? / Simply,* I said/ I've been holding back
the years like I was Simply Red/
I wasn't looking for love/ Love found me
My angel fell from heaven/ It's as simple as can be
I would say simple prayers to God upstairs
I didn't think He was listening/ I didn't think He cared
But with me being a simpleton/ I never left my chair
And now I'm simply walking
I'm simply talking/ I'm simply living my life to the fullest
I'm simply not stopping/ I'm in a simple relationship that
has nothing but love/ I simply love all of our simple kisses
and all of our simple hugs/ Simply stated
I'm a simple man
I want to live a simple life
Marry a simple wife
So we can simply spend 40 simple days
and 40 simple nights...

## SIMPLE

## MY HOUR GLASS

As my thoughts begin to change like HD channels
I grab the closest object to me and I light it like a candle
My heart is dismantled - I close my eyes shut
My love, I see your heart is bleeding - no wounds, no cuts
Deserts divide us and oceans are in between
Your touch is my fire
Your kiss is my steam
Mentally we are one
Spiritually we have begun
To become eye level with God's Son
His love is the light that lights up our life
May His light continue to shine even at night
No living in darkness - We have faith in His might
Blue skies - White smiles - Blue eyes - White towels
White robes - White wine - White clothes - Right time
I love your bright eyes - Look deep - Get lost in my sight
I can see your past in your left and your future in your right
Don't blink - Your lids cause me to sink - Share your desires
My thoughts spin like flat tires - Out of control like a wild fire
***** No body contact - Yet your mind sex has me wired *****
I must have sex on my mind - I assume my due date has expired

"My feelings for you remain so profound, so primal, so real, that
I lack ability to voice them. Why does God feel I am worthy of
one of His angels? I'll never know. But I've learned
never to question His gifts, but instead to
cherish them as I do the air that I breathe."
Cheo Hodari Coker

This is a spiritual love........................Enter into my heart
**BECOME A COMPANION WITH MY SOUL**
Like a seed planted in soil......May our love grow
Unconsciously, I've fallen....................Love can be so deep
I haven't hit the bottom yet
Because emotionally I'm not complete
My emotions, many times have overruled my thoughts
My feelings, many times have overturned my droughts
If love is love, and God is love, then love is God
If I know God, then I must know love
This same love has caused my knees to hit the floor
And my tears to hit the rug
Love has washed away my fears
All these years, cleansed by His blood
Take my hand and walk with me as I walk with Them
Father, Son, and Holy Spirit......Our light is no longer dim
Love is like a mighty tree from God
With many branches and stems
Pick your fruit
The taste of God's grace is a taste we will never lose
His love we will always choose...

# I KNEW I LOVED YOU BEFORE I LOVED YOU

You know how I knew?
By the way the blue birds flew when they saw you
By the way the blades of grass
Straightened their backs when you spoke
By the way the butterflies smiled when they smelled you
By the way the sun warmed my heart when I wrote
**I knew I loved you before I loved you**
You know how I knew?
By the way stars sparkled brightly when I was with you
By the way I blushed when others spoke your sweet name
By the way my prayers became focused on your well being
By the way your joy washed over my pain
**I knew I loved you before I loved you**
You know how I knew?
By the way you edified my manhood when I was stagnate
By the way I respectfully treated you as my friend
By the way the Almighty confirmed His will for our lives
By the way our hearts seemed to naturally blend
**That's how I knew I loved you before I loved you**
That's how I knew you were the one
That's how I knew you were my future
That's how I knew my search was done…

To propose

or

Not to propose

That is the question

If I propose…

I am forever tested

If I oppose…

Then I am forever questioned

So with this being said

**MY DECISION WILL BE…**

*I shall ask my love to marry me!*

Hello in there
I can't wait to meet you
Your name is already chosen
I'm sure it will complete you

You're not even conceived yet
Mama and I haven't sexually met
But you're going to be a wonderful baby
Healthy and blessed

You're going to have a special gift
So beautiful and rare
It will cause those with talents
To envy and stare

My future child to be
Your mama and I love you already
We can't wait to have you
But first we must be married


**SMILE    : 3 )**

## I'M GETTING MARRIED

No children yet

Purposefully abstinent nearly 7 years

My future is set

Our wedding day was prophesied

I'm so glad my lady and I waited

God, You are such a great matchmaker

I pray for Your presence daily

Our marriage - I believe was destined

Time has unveiled Your perfect plan

There is much power in a praying woman

But more power in a praying man

Proverbs - Eighteen: Twenty Two
*"Whosoever finds a wife finds a good thing,
and obtains favor from the Lord."*

## CAN A MAN FIND A WOMAN?

Can a man find a woman who walks in humility and truth?
Is there such a woman with the destiny of Ruth?

Can a man find a woman who sees Jesus in the mirror?
Is there such a woman with the patience of Sarah?

Can a man find a woman who has the ability to tarry?
Is there such a woman with the legacy of Mary?

Can a man find a woman who has two sides to her facial?
Is there such a woman as versatile as Leah and Rachel?

Can a man find a woman as his helpmate and cleave?
Is there such a woman with the suitability of Eve?

Can a man find a woman as priceless as a hidden treasure?
Is there such a woman with the favor of Esther?

Can a man find a woman on this journey called life?
Is there such a woman willing to accept the role of a wife?

I love it when we play…
Complete strangers becoming friends in the length of a day.
I love it when we share…
Ice cream together as the weather stops and stares.
I love it when we laugh…
Seeing you smile externally, internally erases my past.
I love it when we say…
Each other's thoughts out loud like it was pro-phe-say.
I love it when we glare…
Into each other's eyes and run fingers through the hair.
I love it when we crash…
Our chemistry together like boats on a sea moving too fast.
I love it when we pray…
Closing our eyes and asking for God's presence to stay.
I love it when we care…
For the same things, compassionately,
like two doves in the air.
I love it when we passed…
Each other for the first time, because a small voice said…
**IT WILL LAST**

*My very first poem written to my lovely wife, Jasmine*
*8-18-08*

*...* GOD

# GOD...

There is something so powerful about writing from my heart to God, and on the behalf of God to His people, which just so happens to be you. The Lord has given me a gift from my childhood that has not faded away; an ability to put words on paper and write uninhibited with passion. When inspired by my Lord and Savior, the words flow from my heart like a calm waterfall. There is no end to His glorious inspiration. If you are a praying person, pray that my writing ability will continue to prosper as my soul prospers and stays connected to the source of my livelihood, as He speaks, moves, and lives inside of me, so giantly ...

This is my poetry collection of GOD ... Enjoy!

**GOD LOVES ME!**

And that's why I love Him

And that's why I love Me

And that's why I love You

Yesterday I was
**LOOKING**
**DOWN**
from a few thousand feet

In the air

Through my plane's window I stared
My thoughts I will share

How small and insignificant we seem from up there
Merely dots on the ground
Barely found up there

Clouds blocking my view of mountainous mounds up there

Watching the bright sun flare with a glare from up there

Closer to God

Still amazed by how much He cares …

From up there

Don't take Your eyes off me/Please don't ever leave my side/ I'll never let You leave my heart/Although at times You've left my mind/We don't talk like we ought to/We don't spend time like we should/Many times You've treated me like a cell phone, **"CAN YOU HEAR ME NOW? GOOD!"**/Or was it me that was giving You limited minutes/Telling You that I had to go before our conversation was finished/Not calling You back when I said I was gonna/Acting like the number one stunner with no Hummer/With no cheddar/I must've forgot that You keep track of everything I don't remember/From January to December/Fall, winter, spring, and summer/I have Your number and You have mine/Lord, I'll answer - You can call at anytime/Free nights and weekends/Even when I'm sleeping/Buzz me on my cell phone/You don't have to have a reason/We need to catch up/Tell me what's been going on/I know the world is in trouble/I hope no atomic bombs/Let's speak about love, not hate/No more sad songs/I can tell You about my family/My pops and my mom/My brother, sister, and friends, plus all the things I've done wrong/If You're willing to hear my confessions, God, I'm willing to talk long ...

## MY LORD, HOW GREAT THOU ART!

What a blessing it is to have two hearts

My praise rolls over from the night to the morn

By Your amazing grace, I have been re-born

How can a man depart from his mother's womb twice?

"No," You said, "but by the renewing of your minds"

Set free my ears, so I may hear and understand

If I seek, then I shall find - Your perfect will for man

At an early age, I have sought and I have found

So profound my discoveries, my knees hit the ground

I recognize the king that You have called me to be

I put on my bejeweled crown, ever so silently

A wise man remains silent in his prideful ways

I promise I will not make a sound, my silence stays

Though men may rave and women may compliment

My humility deflates my ego, there is no settlement

God, the Bible is my perfect picture, my pilot,

My pavement, my patience, my purpose,

My passion, my peace, my pride,

My push, my shove, my new love

Jesus, thank You for Your spiritual hugs

## IT'S OKAY

I write songs and psalms like David did
I pray long and hard like the Levites' kids

  If I keep my job, it's okay
  If I lose my job, that's even better
No tears in a bucket or on the sleeves of my sweater

  If I keep my car, it's okay
  If I lose my car, it's even better
Matthew 5:45 already predicts my life's weather

  If I keep my life, it's okay
  If I lose my life, it's even better
To be absent in the body is to be present with the Lord
This builds enough confidence in me to write this letter

  God, You are so trustworthy - It assures me
   Knowing You hold my problems in Your palm
    Doesn't worry me - Most certainly

   Your words remain true in my deepest parts
 I don't have the weakest heart, but I know a few that do
  There are a few in my crew that don't trust You
   How can they have faith, but not trust?

  A believer believes, right?
  No matter what
And no matter what means, No Matter What!

I once was blind/ But now I see
The many blessings God has for me
My eyes are open/ They once were shut
He is the reason for the darkness lightening up
My eyesight is narrow/ No longer peripheral
God is my best friend/ And it's more than spiritual
God is real/ And it's more than theoretical
God is magical/ He performs more than miracles
I'm on the outside looking in
Because He knows the middle's full
I can say now that I've heard Him speak
I can say now that I've heard Him teach
All He wants us to do is look up and reach
If I open my mouth wide, God will fill it
Psalms 81:10 keeps it real/ Tell me if you feel it
I've been called to be a witness/ His Glory I shall reveal it
The hand I've been dealt I must deal with it
I can't ask The Dealer to re-deal it/ Absorb my words
I pray you won't appeal it/ Devil, my life you can't steal it
I've been bought by the Lord's blood
I've been filled with the Lord's love
The more I ask for refills, the more He fills my cup
I've never sold drugs/ I've never claimed to be a thug
The one thing I've proclaimed is Jesus' salvation
And the never ending power of…

**GOD'S LOVE**

## ~ <u>(MY FOREVER)</u> ~

"Excuse me, Jesus… Do You have a minute?"
*"I have all the time you need, my child. My time is infinite."*

"Well, I have some questions that my faith can't answer."
*"My dear child, I already know that your aunt has cancer."*

"But, she's losing her hair and her skin is changing colors."
*"I know. I'm waiting for her husband to tell her that he still loves her."*

"You're waiting? Waiting for what?" I asked.
*"O young at heart, my thoughts are higher than yours."*
He laughed.

"But she's dying! Why not just take her now?"
*"I'm testing his love for her. Shhh, we can't be too loud."*

"Jesus, I'm confused. Do You always do this?"
*"It depends on the circumstances I put them in."*

"So my faith isn't good enough to bring my aunt back whole?"
*"This time your faith is not according to my will.
Don't heap coals."*

"So…what should I pray for? Who should receive?"
*"Pray for your uncle, my young child.
In me, he does not believe."*

"He told me once that he used to. What happened there?"
**"*I didn't give him what he asked for.
So now he doesn't care.*"**

"If You don't mind me asking, what did he desire?"
**"*He wanted his father to return to him in his Navy attire*.**"

"His father died too? Did his faith fall short of Your will also?"
**"*Yes. Tell him his father rescued three future apostles*.**"

"Wow. So, our trust in You should surpass our faith, right?"
**"*I'm pleased with both. Let neither one leave my sight.*"**

"I won't. I will tell my aunt and uncle the same."
**"*Tell them that I'm watching them,
and there's a purpose already engraved*.**"

"I will. I will. I'll share with them Your plan," I boasted.
**"*And when you do, I will retrieve her soul into my hand*.**"
He motioned.

"She'll be with You in heaven?!
What a thrill! What a pleasure!"
**"*Yes, my precious child. And what's mine is yours also…
FOREVER*.**"

## MAY WE BE ...

| | |
|---|---|
| The head and not the tail | Deuteronomy 28:13 |
| The blessing and not the curse | Zechariah 8:13 |
| The obedient and not the rebellious | Isaiah 50:5 |
| The boss and not the employee | Genesis 24:34 |
| The teacher and not the student | Hebrews 5:12 |
| The wise and not the foolish | Proverbs 13:20 |
| The saint and not the sinner | Psalms 37:28 |
| The lover and not the fighter | 1 Samuel 16:21 |
| The lender and not the borrower | Deuteronomy 15:6 |
| The strong and not the weak | 2 Chronicles 15:7 |
| The clean and not the dirty | Isaiah 1:16 |
| The winner and not the loser | 1 Corinthians 9:24 |
| The finisher and not the quitter | John 17:4 |
| The healthy and not the sick | Jeremiah 33:6 |
| The humble and not the prideful | 1 Kings 21:29 |
| The answer and not the question | Luke 23:9 |
| Above and not beneath | Deuteronomy 28:13 |
| The swift and not the sluggish | 2 Samuel 1:23 |
| The bold and not the shy | Ephesians 6:20 |
| The courageous and not the fearful | Isaiah 35:4 |
| The sun and not the rain | Matthew 13:43 |

May we be ... the right and not those left! Luke 17:36

**MY SONG**

When I was younger
I had a dream
That I was flying
I would spread my wings and fly
So high amongst the trees
Soaring lightly in the breeze
Singing I'm free
I'm free
I'm free

Now that I am older
I have a dream
That I am living
So abundantly
So vibrantly
I'm alive you see
Because He lives inside of me
So giantly
Singing I'm free
I'm free
I'm free

## YOU HEARD ME!

You actually answered my prayers

My supplications reached Your ears, now I have 31 flavors

No Baskin Robbins over here though

But certainly lots of cake and ice cream

All of this celebrating over my prayers being answered

Makes I scream... Aaaaaaahhhhhhhhh! YES!

Thank You, Jesus!

How did a past relationship become a lifelong lesson?
Who could've imagined my future being my present?
First comes knowledge, then comes understanding,
And then comes wisdom with no baby carriage
God has given me a rainstorm to walk through
I've purged myself of all the evil spirited tattoos
I embrace what I've learned as a lesson well earned
I cried tears at the time/ But my life turned out fine
I think God knew all along where I'd stand years later
I'm singing praiseworthy songs/ Jesus is my Savior
I'm His servant and friend/ Family member 'til the end
He's my big brother/ My teacher and counselor
He's my big boss/ My preacher and high tower
My stepping stone and high mountain
My ever-flowing fountain
My never ending bread of life
The giver of sight
All victories and no defeats
He is my peace/My righteousness
My craftiness and my creative ways
He's the potter/I'm the clay
He is the True Vine and I am the branch
He is the light and I am the lamp
My shepherd/My lion/My lamb
The Great I AM
**HUMBLY I STAND**
I'm nothing without You, Jesus
You are the significance within my soul
Thank You for closing the gap between us
My propitiation/ My revelation
Your Gospel is my education
I study to show myself approved
Just the mere thought of Your Kingdom
Changes my moods!

### *WHO CAN SEE?*

I'm clothed in glory ~ My clothes are holy
Not like the holes you can see through
But whole like completely true
Allow Me to complete you and make you holy too
My Father is Elohim ~ My Brother is Jesus
The three of Us make a holy trinity
No wrinkles ~ All creases
We are sharp ~ Our tongue is like a two edged sword
Before the start We were one ~ You can call Us The Lord
We are one ~ You can call Us the Word
Open your eyes and recognize the Fruit of the Spirit is Me
Supernaturally I give sight to the blind
Still I wonder who can see?

When you abide in Me ~ It is I who abides in you
When you abuse your body ~ I can feel it too
I'm crying on the inside of you and I bet you had no clue
I become displeased when I'm compressed
I tell you the truth
You keep Me concealed like I'm an illegal weapon
Don't you know that I'm quicker than the speed of light and I
should be used every available second?

I give you strength when you have none
I'm the grace that provides blessings
I'm the anointing that descends like a dove
I'm the mercy that provides lessons
I'm the gift that My Father wants to give you so freely
Open your eyes and recognize the Fruit of the Spirit is Me
Supernaturally I give sight to the blind
Still I wonder who can see?

~ I can see you ~
Even when My eyes are closed like windows
My eyelids are like crystal clear glass
Seeing Me is like watching the wind blow
You see Me but you don't
~ You feel Me ~
I give you chills when it's not even cold
~ You smell Me ~
I was the breath that was blown into Adam's nose
~ You hear Me ~
I'm the edifying voice
You faintly hear echoing in your dome
~ You taste Me ~
Scripture proclaims that I'm good for your bones
Man cannot live on bread alone
But on every spoken word that proceeds
Out of the mouth of God
Without Me, your life would be three times as hard
Don't live your life behind spiritual bars
Open your eyes and recognize the Fruit of the Spirit is Me
Supernaturally I give sight to the blind
Still I wonder, who can see?
~ Who can see? ~

# I STRUGGLE

I can't even lie
There's a sinful magnetic pull, pulling at my eyes
Pulling at my heart
Pulling at my mind
Lust is a bad habit that whispers in my ears
Sometimes temptation and opportunity
Are heard so loud
They are the only things I hear
Lord, tell me why lust is so hard to break
I constantly get delivered
But is my deliverance real or fake?
Fiction or non-fiction? Small or great?
Shake my sins away until I feel awake
Am I still deep in my sleep?
I still feel deep in my sins
I know obedience is Your will, but remind me again
Even a righteous man is forgiven a multitude of times
Forgive me seventy times seven, Lord
Cleanse my heart - Renew my mind

## I'M WEARY

Will my groaning ever end?
I water my couch with tears
I cry rivers in my bed

Only God
Has heard the voice of my weeping
My eyes are consumed with grief
I find no peace when I'm sleeping

No Mercy
Life spits in my face while I'm down
Nevertheless, my attempt to arise is fulfilled
Strength is gained for another round

His Grace
Empowers me with a second wind
I wipe the tears from my face
Ready to contend with life again

## JUST IN HART

<pre>
          *****              *****
       Such a heart      You've given me
      With a God shaped hole to be filled
    It is my cave of love that goes deeper than wells
 Such compassion for others; a package created for You
     No more selfish desires of not wanting to be used
      The heart of man is deceitful beyond all things
    Out of the abundance of my heart my mouth speaks
  God, I long to be used (      ) by my Lord and Savior
       ****** He is greater than my heart *****
       *** Every one of my four chambers ***
          Listen to the beating of my heart
              The loud thumping within
              My heart pumps blood for ink
                It records every sin
                 Again and again
                **********
                   *******
                      **
</pre>

My voice yells up to Your heavenly throne
Jesus, I know You're listening - You can hear every moan
Take over this body - my mind, my soul, and my heart
It is by divine selection that my name... is Justin Hart

The Lord has given me **THE ABILITY TO WRITE** with delight/ I speak freely with my pen/ I flow like cursive writing *italicized*, my friend/ Who could've predicted my future being my present?/ "Certainly, not I," said the young man with penmanship/ My passion for writing is an immeasurable gift from above/ Still, if I wrote a dozen love letters to heaven everyday it wouldn't equal up/ So the best I will do is share my letters with the world/ I've been chosen from my birth/ No need for a referral/ He writes for me when I'm isolated/ My focus on Him has become concentrated/ There's no more debating it/ Colored ink is merely words trapped in my pen/ There are 26 letters in the alphabet/ Where shall I begin?/ Breathe life into my writing utensils, however You wish/ What I start, I will finish/ I'm Popeye without the spinach/ I know food is for the stomach, but may Your grace feed my lineage/ Am I asking for too much or not enough?/ I'm not asking for good luck, but The Potter's touch/ You can use my hands for Your glory/ Liquid Sunshine/ You've already given me an awesome testimony/ My Jesus/ You are so, so worthy/ I refuse to let my pride get it confused/ But some days You make me feel like I can out rhyme all of Langston Hughes' nephews… I'm a writer!

### S. A. V. E. D.

**S** - Soon after subtle reminders of my sinful side my stupid pride still struggles to succumb to second place in my life but I slowly realize just how strong my Savior is on the inside and I guess it's because He's never died so in sequence I'm alive a second time

**A** - Already absent minded of my decision to remain abstinent to sin I forget my answers to why abstract thoughts continue to allure me in adjacent directions that always cause me to bend yet attentively I battle with them and anticipate my spirit man to win - again

**V** - Very good possibility that Satan's worldly venom has been strategically used to destroy my God given spirit-powered vehicle better known as my temple or God's vessel, which nowadays very seldom violates His verbal commandments which wasn't always the case back in my V-neck days

**E** - Every now and again it's imperative that I empty out my earth - my earth is my world - my world is everything I embrace so I can eclipse the Son's essence in order to elevate the existence of Him who lives within me so extravagantly

**D** - Death is different than death so I desire the first over the latter which makes sense to me now because I'm young, however dead, yet still alive because I've denied myself of my dog-like flesh which craves all the lustful things that I now despise - ever since I got S.A.V.E.D.

**MY ILLNESS**

They call it a thorn in the flesh
They say, "It must be God's will."
But I call it a temporary issue
I say, "I'm far from being ill."

They call it a disease, or even a sickness
They say, "It's a consequence of sin."
But I call my issue God's problem
I say, "My struggle is all His."

The blood, the bones, the organs, the skin
The heart, the lungs, the breasts, the ribs
The eyes, the nose, the ears, the head
The brain, the back, the knees, the legs

They call my condition chronic
They say, "It's terminal."
But I call it temporary
I say, "It's curable."

They call it unfortunate
They say, "Just accept it."
But I call on prayer
I say, "My words are my greatest weapon."

Tropical rain forests
Exotic birds lined up
Like a chorus
Palm trees and coconuts
Almond colored shores
Vibrant plants, flowers
And more
Delicious fruits
And vegetables
Flat prairie plains
Cracking dry deserts
No sign of rain
Underwater caves
Mountains
Stretching for miles
Boulders, rocks
Pebbles at bottom
Orange leaves in autumn
Thick fog and icicles
In winter
Pure untouched snow priceless
Beautiful sunrises
And sunsets
Rainbows stretched
In the midst
White cumulous clouds
Blue skies speak so loud
One full moon
That lights up the night
Oceans and seas
With no end in sight
Rivers that never run dry

The expansion
Of the Grand Canyon
The cool breeze of wind
Diamonds, crystals
Gold, gems
All of this
Reflects the glory of Him
The massive size of icebergs
The rumbling
Sound of volcanoes
Lightning
And rolling thunder
The whirling fear of tornados
Hurricanes
And crashing waves
Crumbling earthquakes
**GOD CREATED IT ALL**
Waterfalls and all
Roaring lions, elephants
And whales
Human beings
Male and female
The immensity
Of our brain and eyes
The brain
Has 4 million pain alerts
The eyes
Have 2 million active parts
4 quarts of human blood
Have 22 trillion cells
And you are going to tell me
That God is not real???

# ...I'M A WRITER

(Bonus Material)

When you look in the mirror, understand that God's most beautiful work came from the dirt.

Purity
In its purest form
Isn't purer than
The purest One
Jesus!

Goodness gracious, stop using God's name in vain.
If you have nothing good to say ... He's not the one to blame.

Amazing! Before Coming Down, Eternity Fought. God Hallowed. I, Jesus, Kept Loving Man. Nothing Opposed Perfection's Quest. Reality Settled. This Universal Victory Will X-amine Your Zeal.

God, sometimes I think You wrote the Bible specifically for me.

When I read it, it speaks specifically to me.

I Love You, Lord!

Writers write, right?

So since I am, I will write.

I will write with no lights; eyes closed and no sight.

I will write every single day and every single night.

I might. I will. Write with much passion and skill… I repeat, with much skill and passion. Write in cursive like my pen was plastic. Inscription, **bold,** *italicized*, <u>underlined.</u> I write circumcised. No shame at all. No shame when I call on the Lord for inspiration. I tackle hurdles in my life that I'm facing. Much patience with patients. No mercy for the merciless. No favor for those without flavor.

I write as though your life depended on it.

Call me a life saver. My ink illuminates the page.

Turn it sideways. Watch it glow…

### *I'M A WRITER!*

Floetry
I flow like ancient typography
My style is calligraphy
I harmonize like a symphony
Simply – I flow

Floetry
I flow like water streams in the spring, lingering
Hot like a summer breeze, sizzling
No need to mimic me
I'll flow until you're sick of me – I flow

Floetry
You think you know me but your knowledge is hardly
I flow like a bloody nose on the concrete
Listen to me speak - I flow

Floetry
I flow like those ladies, cordially
Morally, I rhyme for the Lord of lord's you see
I'm going door to door with meat
Have a seat – I flow

Floetry
I flow like the wind blows when it's snowing
Cold like a frost bitten nose glowing
Red like the carpet I walk on
Show boating
My pen's smokin' - I flow

**I'M A WRITER!**

Sweet peace surrounds me like whispers in the night

Soft words lift me high like warm embraces take flight

I melt internally

From the cold heart You've transplanted

God, Your eyes burn with flames

I anticipate Your earth's landing

What a blend Your ingredients make with my soul

Such a taste to unfold from my wrapper of gold

I believe Jesus died for the sins of the world

He liberates my spirit man

Like an oyster frees it's pearl…

***I'M A WRITER!***

I'm a writer/ On fire/ It's like lightning when I strike/ My thunder hits your ears in silence when I write/ Ignite your ability to stroke the paper with ink/ Girls wink at the pleasure of me writing what I think/ I stink so good, would you agree?/ It hurts so good to believe in a being that created human beings after trees/ The birds in the sky/ The fish in the sea/ The Creator gives creativity so creatively/ My writing ability comes from a source outside of myself/ He's the supplier of my health and wealth/ He makes my heart melt/ It's on fire...

### *I'M A WRITER!*

Do I dare exercise my pen and write for You?

Lord, do You prefer Free Flow, Rhythmic

Blank Verse, Epic, or Haiku?

My poetry is written directly aimed at Your heart, God

I know You will receive it with a smile every time

And that's the bottom line, huh?

My tongue is the pen of a ready writer

Let freedom ring, like I'm a freedom fighter

Who said worshipping You has to be through prayer only?

Watch the ink in my pen dissipate slowly...

***I'M A WRITER!***

*Together*
*Life is not so complicated*
*Forever*
*Love should be re-instated*
*God's grace is so amazing*
*The cumulous clouds read painted...*

*Life, Love & God*

CPSIA information can be obtained at www.ICGtesting.com
Printed in the USA
LVOW040718140113

315541LV00001B/2/P

9 780983 354482